EASYWAY GUIDES

A GUIDE
TO
WRITING YOUR OWN WILL
THE EASYWAY
JAMES GRANT

© Straightforward Publishing 2009

British Cataloguing in Publication data. A catalogue record is available for this book from the British Library.

ISBN 9781847161 31 4

Printed in the United Kingdom by GN Press Essex

Cover Design by Bookworks Islington

CONTENTS

SECTION 1. THE FORMATION OF A WILL

....

....

....

SECTION TWO-ADMINISTRATION OF ESTATES

....

1

Producing a Will

The main principle underlying any will is that, if you have possessions, or any other assets, then you need to organise a will which will ensure that chosen people benefit after your death.

In the majority of cases, a person's affairs are relatively uncomplicated and should not involve the use of a solicitor.

There are certain basic rules to be followed in the formation of a will and if they are then it should be legally binding.

The only inhibiting factor on the disposal of your assets will be any tax liability following death, which will be dealt with later in this book.

There are a number of other factors to consider, however:

- Age of person making a will

A will made by anyone under the age of eighteen, known as a minor, will not be valid unless that person is a member of the services (armed forces) and is on active service.

- Mental health considerations

A will formed by a person, who was insane at the time of writing, will not be valid. Mental illness in itself is not a barrier to creating a will, as long as proof can be shown that the person was not insane at the time of writing. Subsequent mental illness, following the formation of a will, will not be a barrier to a will's validity.

- Definition of insanity

Insanity, or this particular condition, will normally apply to anyone certified as such and detained in a mental institution. In addition, the Mental Health Act covers those in " a state of arrested or incomplete development of mind which includes sub-normality of intelligence and is of such a nature or degree that the patient is incapable of living an independent life or guarding against serious exploitation.

In any situation where there is doubt as to a persons capabilities then it is always best to have any will validated by an expert. This applies to anyone, not just those classified as insane.

The main point of any will is that, in the final analysis, a court would have to be satisfied that the contents of the will are genuine, there has not been any attempt whatsoever to alter the contents or to influence that persons mind. The person writing the will must have fashioned its contents with no outside interference.

Unfortunately, the history of the production of people's last will and testament is littered with greedy and unscrupulous persons who wish to gain from another's demise. It is necessary to be careful!

Illiteracy

Although the person leaving the will (testator) has to be able to understand what he or she is doing when they make a will, there is no requirement that they are capable of reading the will. Someone who cannot read or write may make a valid will by dictating their wishes to a person to write down. The testator docs not even have to be able to write their own name. The law allows them to 'make their mark' usually by making a cross, instead of signing the will.

Physical disability

Physical disability does not prevent a person from making a will. If the testator is capable of making their wishes understood, then even those with very severe disabilities can make a will. For example, if someone has been paralysed and is unable to sign, they may still make a will. Equally, a person who is blind may make a will. In these cases the law allows the testator to tell another person to sign the will, but that signing must take place in the testators presence.

The reasons for making a will

The main reason for making a will is to ensure that you make the choice as to who you leave your possessions, and not the state. You can also impose any specific conditions you want in your will.

For example, you can impose age conditions or conditions relating to the need to perform certain duties before benefiting.

If you do not make a will then, on your death, the law of intestacy will apply to the disposal of your estate. You will have had no say and certain criteria are applied by the state, which will take responsibility.

In the circumstances described above, after costs such as funeral and administration of other aspects of death, an order of preference is established, as follows:

- Your spouse, which is your husband or wife
- Any children you may have. This includes all children, whether by marriage, illegitimate or adopted.
- Parents
- Brothers and sisters
- Half brothers or sisters
- Grandparents
- Uncles and aunts
- Uncles and aunts (half blood)

It is the law of intestacy that if any of the above, in that order, die before the person who is the subject of intestacy, then their children will automatically benefit in their place.

There are conditions which will affect the above order of beneficiaries:

- If the spouse of a person is still living and there are no surviving children, parents, brothers or sisters or any of their offspring living then the spouse will benefit solely

- If the spouse is still living and there is children, the estate will be divided along the following lines:

The spouse will take all the personal items and up to £75,000 if money is involved. This will be augmented by interest on the money from the date of death. There will be a life interest in half of the residue of the estate. This means use as opposed to ownership. In the case of money it relates to interest on capital only and not the capital itself;

Children (equal shares) Half the residue of the estate plus the other half on the death of the spouse.

If the spouse is still alive, there are no children but there are other relatives, such as parents, brothers and sisters and their children the following rules apply:

The spouse will have all the personal items and up to £125000 if it is available, interest on money and half the residue of the estate.

Parents will receive half the residue or, if there are no parents alive then brothers and sisters will, in equal shares, keep half the residue.

By law, the spouse is entitled to carry on living in the matrimonial home after death. The matrimonial home is defined as the place where he or she had been living at the time of death. If there is no spouse living but there are children then the estate will be divided equally between them. This will occur when they are over the age of eighteen or marry, whichever occurs first.

If there is no spouse and no children but there are parents, then the estate will be divided equally between them.

If there is no spouse, no children and no parents, then the estate will be divided equally between brothers and sisters.

If there are no brothers and sisters then half brothers and sisters. If none, grandparents. If not, uncles and aunts and if none to half blood uncles and aunts.

As can be seen, the law of intestacy tries to ensure that at least someone benefits from a person's possessions on death. There is a ranking order and in most cases there would be someone to benefit.

There are certain categories of person who fall outside of the law of intestacy, even though there may have been some connection in the past:

Divorced and separated persons

There is no right of entitlement whatsoever for a divorced person to benefit from an estate on death. This right ceases from the decree absolute.

If a separation order is granted by a divorce court then there is no entitlement to benefit. If the separation is informal and there is separate habitation or a Magistrates court order has been granted for separation then there is normal entitlement.

Cohabitation

The law of intestacy dictates that, if you were living with someone, but not married, at the time of death, then that person has no direct claim to the estate. However, in practice this operates somewhat differently and there is a law, Provision for Family and Dependants Act 1975 under which cohabitees can claim. We will be discussing this a little later.

Although anyone has a right to have their estate distributed in accordance with the law of intestacy it is highly inadvisable. It is better at all time to ensure that you have complete control over where your money goes. It may be that you do not wish immediate family to benefit over others and that you wish to leave all your money to a particular favoured person or to an institution. This can only be achieved by personalising your will and remaining in control of what happens after your death.

****

2

When to
Produce a Will

It is essential that you make a will as soon as possible. If you leave it, there is a chance that you may never get round to doing it and may be reliant upon the state doing it for you. There is also the chance that you will leave a situation where people start to contest your possessions, fight amongst each other and fall out.

There are many things to consider when you decide to produce a will. As a person gets older, chances are that he or she will become wealthier. Savings grow, endowments increase, insurance policies become more valuable, property is purchased and so on. A bank balance in itself is no indicator of worth, as there are many other elements which add up to wealth.

Changes in personal circumstances often justify the need to make a will.

- Ownership of property
- Children
- Marriage or remarriage
- Employment
- Illness

- Divorce and separation
- Increase in personal wealth, such as an inheritance

Ownership of property

Ownership of property usually implies a mortgage. If you are wise it will also imply life insurance to at least the value of the property. It is very prudent to make a will which specifies exactly to whom the property will be left. As we have seen, the law of intestacy provides for the decision if you do not have a will.

Children

As we have seen, under the law of intestacy, any children you have will benefit after your death. However, it is very sensible, under a will, to specify how and when they will benefit. It could be that you may let someone else make that decision later on. Whatever, you should make it very clear in your will.

Marriage or remarriage

The most important point to remember is that marriage or remarriage will automatically revoke the provisions of any former will, although this is not the case in Scotland. Therefore, when marrying you should make certain that your will is up to date and that you have altered the provisions. In short, you should amend your will, or produce a new will in order to outline clearly what you want your new partner to have.

Employment

You should be very aware that certain types of employment carry greater risks than others. This will necessitate producing a will as soon as possible as if you are in a high-risk category then you need to ensure that those nearest you are catered for.

Illness

Illness is something that none of us want but cannot avoid if it decides to strike. No matter how healthy you are you should take this into account when considering putting together a will. In addition, some people have a family history of illness and chances are that they too could suffer. Therefore illness is a very real motivator for producing a will.

Divorce and separation

The law of intestacy states that if you die your divorced spouse loses all rights to your estate. You may not want this to happen and make provisions in your will. Although children of any marriage will benefit it could be that you may wish to make slightly different provisions for different children.

Increase in personal wealth

Financial success, and inheritance will increase your wealth and inevitably make you estate more complicated. It is absolutely essential to ensure that you have a will and that you are updating that will regularly to take into account increased assets.

The provisions of a will

Having considered some of the many reasons for producing a will, it is now necessary to look at exactly what goes into a will.

Essentially, the purpose of a will is to ensure that everything you have accumulated in your life is disposed of in accordance with your own desires. The main areas to consider when formulating a will are:

- Money you have saved, in whatever form
- Any buildings (property) you have
- Any land you have
- Any insurance policies you have. This is of utmost importance
- Any shares you may own
- Trusts set up
- Any other personal effects

Money you have saved

Money is treated as part of your wider estate and will automatically go to those named as the main beneficiaries. However, you might wish to make individual bequests to other people outside your family. These have to be specified. When including any provisions in your will relating to money, you should be very clear about the whereabouts of any saving accounts or endowments, premium bonds etc. Life becomes very difficult if you have left sums of money but there is no knowledge of the

whereabouts of this. Inevitably, solicitors have to be employed and this becomes very expensive indeed.

Property

It is necessary to make provisions for any property you have. If you are the sole owner of a property then you can dispose of it as you wish. Any organisation with a superior interest would take an interest, particularly if there are mortgages outstanding. It is important to remember that if you are a joint owner of a property, such as a joint tenancy, then on death this joint ownership reverts to the other joint owner, bringing it into sole ownership. Leasehold property can be different only in so much as the executor of an estate will usually need permission before assigning a lease. This can be obtained from the freeholder.

Land

Although the same principles apply to land as to property, indeed often the two are combined, in certain circumstances land may be owned separately. In this case the land and everything on it can be left in the will.

Insurance policies

The contents of any insurance policy needs to be checked carefully. In certain cases there are restrictions on who can benefit on death. Particular people may be specified and you have no alternative but to let such people benefit, even though your own circumstances may have changed. If there are no restrictions then you can bequeath any money as you see fit.

Shares and trusts

Shares can normally be bequeathed in a will as anything else. However, depending on the type of share, it is just possible that there may be restrictions. One such situation is where shares are held in a private company and there may be a buy back clause.

Trusts can be set up for the benefit of family and friends. However, a trust, by its very nature is complex as the law dealing with trusts is complex. It is absolutely essential, if you are considering setting up a trust to get specialist advice.

Personal effects

Although you are perfectly entitled to leave specific items of personal effects in your will, such legacies are separate from those of other possessions such as money or land. The law recognises that in some cases there may not be enough money to pay expenses related to your death. Any money owed will be retrieved from any financial gifts you have outlined. However, personal effects cannot be touched if you have clearly identified these in your will. This includes items of value such as jewelry. It is not enough to be general on this point. You must specify exactly what it is you are leaving and to whom. Remember, certain gifts will be taxable. We will be covering this later in the book under taxation.

The funeral

It is common practice to include such matters as how you wish to be buried, in what manner and the nature of the ceremony, in your will. You should discuss these arrangements with your next

of kin in addition to specifying them in your will as arrangements may be made for a funeral before details of a will are made public. Another way is to detail your wishes in a letter and pass this on to your executor to ensure that the details are known beforehand.

There is no reason why any of your instructions should not be carried out, subject to the law. However, your executor can override your wishes if necessary and expedient.

You can, in addition, make known your wishes for maintenance of your grave after your death. Agreement of the local authority, or relevant burial authority must be sought and there is no obligation on them to do this. In addition, there is a time limit of 99 years in force.

The use of your body after death

It could be that you have decided to leave your body for medical research or donate your organs. This can be done during your final illness, in writing or in front of a minimum of two witnesses. You should contact your local hospital or General Practitioner about this, they will supply you with more details.

Making a recital

A recital consists of a statement at the end of your will which explains how and why you have drawn up a will in the way you have. This is not commonly done but sometimes may be necessary, especially if you have cut people out of your will but do not intend to cause confusion or hurt.

Recitals are sometimes necessary in order to clarify a transfer of authority to others on your death. This could be in business for example. In addition, you may wish to recognise someone's contribution to your life, for example a long serving employee or a particular friend.

3

Provisions In
Your Will

Who to name

When including persons, or organisations, in your will it is better to form a separate list right at the outset.

Naming individuals in your will

There are certain criteria which apply when naming individuals in a will, although in principle you can name who you want. Any person considered an adult, i.e. over 18, can benefit from your will. However, if a person cannot be traced within a time period of seven years after being named, or dies before you, then the amount left in your will to that person is included in what is known as the residue of your estate, what is left after all bequests. You can also make a bequest in your will to cover that eventuality, that is for another named person to benefit in his or her place.

If the bequest is to your own children or any other direct descendant and they die before you then the gift will automatically go to their children, unless there is something to the contrary in your will. In addition, if you make a gift to two or more people and one dies then that share is automatically passed to the other (joint owner).

Children

You are entitled to leave what you want in your will to children whether they are illegitimate or stepchildren. Stepchildren should be stipulated in your will. If children are under 18 then it will be probably necessary to leave property such as land, in trust for them until they reach 18 or any other age stated in the will. No child under 18 can be a trustee.

Those people who are not British citizens, i.e. foreigners can benefit from your will in the same way as anyone else. The only real restriction to this is if there is a state of war between your own country and theirs, in which case it will be necessary to wait until peace is declared.

Mental illness

There is nothing currently in law which prevents a person suffering mental illness from receiving a bequest under a will. Obviously, depending on the state of mind of that person it could be that someone may have to accept the gift and take care of it on the person's behalf.

Bankruptcy

If a person is either bankrupt or facing bankruptcy then if that person receives a gift there is a chance that it could end up in the hands of a creditor. To avoid this happening you can establish a protective trust which will enable the person in receipt of the gift to enjoy any interest arising from the gift during a specific time.

Animals

It is possible to leave money to animals for their care and well being. There is a time limit involved for receipt of the money, which is currently a period of 21 years.

Groups

There is no problem legally with leaving money and other gifts to groups or organisations. However, it is necessary to ensure that the wording of the will is structured in a certain way. It is necessary to understand some of the legislation concerning charities, in order that your bequest can be deemed charitable.

Leaving money/gifts to charities

Many people leave bequests to charity. Major charities often give advice to individuals and other organisations on how to do that. Smaller charities can pose a problem as they may not be as sound and as well administered as larger ones. It is best to stipulate an alternative charity in the event of the smaller one ceasing to operate. If for whatever reason you bequest cannot be passed on to the group concerned then it will be left in the residue of your estate and could be liable to tax. There are a number of causes which might be deemed as charitable. These are:

- Educational causes
- Help for the community
- Animal welfare
- Help for the elderly
- Disabled

31

- Religious groups
- Sick, such as hospices

In the event of making a bequest to a charitable cause, it is certain that you will need expert advice, as with the setting up of trusts.

****

4

Trusts

A trust is a legal arrangement where one group of people called 'trustees' take responsibility for property for the benefit of another group of people called beneficiaries. Trusts come into existence in all sorts of circumstances. A person can create a trust during their lifetime (when they are called the 'settlor') or on death by their will. Trusts are used for a number of things, such as:

- To prevent assets, particularly family assets from being wasted
- To enable property, usually land, to be held for a child. The law says that a person under 18 is incapable of holding legal title to land.
- To provide pensions to former employees and others
- To operate unit trusts and other similar investment vehicles

Is a trust necessary?

In the context of will making, it is not usually necessary to create a trust for a non-residuary gift. Broadly speaking, there are three situations where a trust is needed when considering a gift of residue.

Children

If you intend to make a residuary gift of any sort of property to a child, a trust is necessary because the law does not allow a child to give a valid receipt to your personal representatives or to hold legal title to land.

Life interests

Sometimes, a testator wants to tie up property in order to give one person, usually called the 'life tenant' the right to enjoy that property during their lifetime and, on their death, to make an outright gift of the property to someone else. The most common interests are a right to occupy property.

Contingent interests

The interests in a beneficiary in property is called 'contingent' if his interest in or entitlement to that property is conditional upon the happening of an event.

A contingent interest needs to be distinguished from a 'vested interest'. The interest of a beneficiary in property is called 'vested' if his entitlement to that interest is immediate.

Different types of trust

There are many different types of trust. Generally speaking, will making is concerned with three sorts.

The discretionary trust

This is a trust under which the trustees have discretion about how the monies are spent. Very often, the degree of discretion is wide so that who gets what is entirely a matter for the trustees. Discretionary trusts are a useful tax-planning tool for married couples.

The accumulation and maintenance trust

This special sort of trust is suitable for making future financial provision for your children and for grandchildren. Such trusts enjoyed privileged income tax.

They are so called because this is a trust where the beneficiaries have a clear right to the use of property.

If a trust is required, the trustees should have all the powers they need to enable them to carry out their duties efficiently.

Trustees powers

Trustees powers (and their duties and obligations) come from three sources: Acts of Parliament, general law and the document creating the trust.

5

Preparing a Will

The writing of a will and the way you word it, is of the utmost importance and it is here that skill is needed. If you word the will wrongly then it can be contested, rejected and your estate could be administered by the state.

As long as you observe certain rules then there is no reason why you should go wrong, however.

One of the key rules is that there should be nothing in your will that can be ambiguous or open to interpretation. It is essential to ensure that your intentions are crystal clear. It will probably be necessary to get someone else to look at your will to ensure that it is understood by others.

Preparation of will

A will can of course be rewritten. However, it is very important indeed to ensure that you have spent enough time in the initial preparation stages of your will as it could be enacted at any time, in the event of sudden death. If your possessions are numerous then it is highly likely that the preparation stage will be fairly lengthy as the dividing up will take more thought. This gets more complicated depending on your other circumstances, such as whether you are married or single, have children, intend to leave money to organizations, etc.

You need to make a clear list of what it is you have in order to be able to achieve clarity in your will. For example, property and other possessions will take in any buildings and land you own plus money in various accounts or other forms of saving. In addition there could be jewelry and other valuables to take into account. It is necessary to quantify the current value of these possessions. It is also necessary to balance this out by making a list of any outstanding loans/mortgages or other debts you may have. Funeral costs should come into this. It is essential that you do not attempt to give away more than you actually have and also to deduce any tax liabilities from the final amount after debts. The wording of any will is always done with tax liability in mind.

Listing those who will benefit from your will

Making a list of beneficiaries is obviously necessary, including all groups, individuals and others who will benefit. With each beneficiary you should list exactly what it is that you bequeath. If a trust is necessary, then note this and note down the name of proposed trustees. These persons should be in agreement before being named. Contact any charities that will benefit. They can supply you with a legacy clause to include in your will.

The most important point, at this stage, is that you ensure that what you are leaving does not exceed the estate and that, if liable for tax, then there is sufficient left over to meet these liabilities.

Make a note of any recitals that you wish to include in your will and exactly what you wish to say.

The choice of an executor of your will

The job of any executor is to ensure that your will is administered in accordance with the terms therein as far as is legally possible at that time. It is absolutely essential to ask those people if they consent to being an executor. They may well refuse which could pose problems. You can ask friends or family or alternatively you can ask a solicitor or your bank. They will make a charge for this. However, they are much less likely to make a mistake in the execution of the will than an untrained individual. They will charge and this should be provided for.

If you do choose to appoint an untrained executor, then it is good policy to appoint at least two in order to ensure that there is an element of double-checking and that there are enough people to fulfill the required duties.

The presentation of your will

You can either prepare your will on ordinary sheets of paper or used specially prepared forms which can be obtained from stationers or book shops. Bookshops will usually sell "will packs" which take you through the whole preparation stage, from contemplation to completion. Try to avoid handwriting your will. If it cannot be read then it will be invalid. You should always try to produce it on a word processor or typewriter. This can be more easily altered at any time.

The advantage of using a pre-printed form is that it has all of the required phrases on it and you just fill in the blanks. It just may be that you are not in the position to write your will, as you may be one of the considerable numbers of people who cannot read or write in this country. In this case, you can get someone else to write it for you although it is essential that you understand the contents. Get someone else, independent of the person who wrote it to read it back to you to ensure that the contents reflect your wishes.

The wording of a will

The wording of a will is of the utmost importance as it is absolutely necessary to ensure that you produce a clear document which is an instrument of your own will. The following are some words, which appear in wills, with an explanation of their precise meaning and pitfalls:

"Beneficiary"
this means someone or something that benefits as a result of a gift in a will.
"Bequeath"
"I bequeath" in a will usually refers to personal property such as personal property and money.
"Children"
this includes both legitimate and illegitimate children and also adopted children. Where a gift is to a child and that child has children and dies before the death of the person making the will then the gift will pass on to the child or children of that child if

they are living at the time of the testators death unless an intention to the contrary appears in the will. "Children" does not usually include stepchildren and if you wish a stepchild to be included then this will need to be specified. Children will include stepchildren where there are only step-children alive at the time of making the will.

"Children" can also include grandchildren where it is clear that this was intended or there are only grandchildren and no other children are alive at the date of making a will. You should always specify grandchildren when you want them included.

"Descendants" this means children, grandchildren, great grandchildren and so on down the line. A gift using this word is sometimes phrased "to my descendants living at my death" which includes all those who are alive at the time of the death of the person making a will. Male descendants means males who are descended from females as well as those who are descended from males. A gift to descendants means that they all take equal shares. If you wish each merely to take in default of a parent or parents (e.g. if a parent predeceases you) then add the words "per stirpes".

"Devise"

"I devise" in a will usually refers to a gift of land, which includes a house.

"Executor/Executrix"

this is the person or persons you appoint to administer your will and to carry out your wishes as expressed in your will. Anyone can be appointed an executor, usually expressed as a clause in your will. The few exceptions are those of a minor and those of unsound mind. Solicitors and banks can also be appointed.

Executors can also receive gifts under the will. The executor cannot charge fees, banks and solicitors do but the will must stipulate this. Because of the fact that executors can change their minds about taking on the task of administering your will, it is often better to have two.

"Family"

this word should not be used if it can be helped as it has been interpreted in several different ways. It is, by and large, far to general.

"Husband"this means the husband at the time of making the will. In the event of a divorce, a person remains married until the decree absolute has been granted. Divorce alters the will in so far as any appointment of a former spouse as an executor becomes void, as do any bequests to that person, unless there is a contrary intention in the will.

Generally, if a marriage splits up it is best to review the provisions of a will.

"Infant"

this means a child under the age of eighteen. Land is given to trustees (usually) if left to those under eighteen, as an infant cannot hold an estate in land.

"Issue"

this means all descendants but has been interpreted as having several meanings. In a simple will its use should be avoided altogether as again, it is far too general.

"Minor"

this has the same meaning as infant.

"Nephews"

the meaning of this term depends upon the context of the will. It is far safer, in any such general situation to be specific and name names.

"Next of kin"

this means the closest blood relation.

"Nieces"

the same applies as for nephews.

"Pecuniary legacy"

this means a gift of money in a will.

"Residue"

this means the amount that is left of your estate after effect has been given to all the gifts in your will and testamentary and other expenses have been paid.

"Survivor"

this may apply to persons who are not born at the time of the will. Therefore, a gift to all those who survive a person leaving the will could include all brothers and sisters not yet born.

"Testamentary expenses"

in a will the residue of an estate may be left to a person after all expenses. This includes all known expenses, such as the costs of administering the will.

"Trustee"

a trustee is someone entrusted to look after property for another until a certain age is attained or condition fulfilled. There should always be more than one trustee with two being a usual number.

"Wife"

this means the wife at the time of making the will. Again, in the event of a divorce, then the decree absolute must be granted before that person ceases to be a wife.

Safekeeping of a will

A will must always be kept safe and should be able to be located at the time of your death. You may spend a great deal of time on your will. However, if it cannot be found then it will be assumed that you have not made one.

Any will or codicil may be deposited with your solicitor, if you have one. They will send you an envelope in which to deposit your will. Seal it and complete the information on the outside, giving your name and the details of your executors. Then sign the outside of the sealed envelope in the presence of a witness. Keep a copy of your will in case you want to refer to its contents and then send in the sealed envelope with a covering letter. You will be given an official certificate that the will has been deposited and it is important that you tell your executors this.

6

Contents Of a Will

When writing a will, there is a recognised format which must be followed for the will to be deemed legal. The following constitutes the basic outline:

- A will states that this is your last will and testament
- Your full name and address must be on the will and the date of the will
- All previous wills, if they exist, must be revoked in writing
- There must be an appointment and payment of executors
- Provision for the appointment of a firm of solicitors, if appropriate
- The method of disposal of your body, whether by cremation or burial or whether you have chosen to leave your body for medical purposes. This is not essential
- Payment of testamentary expenses
- Payment of inheritance tax if you are giving gifts free of tax
- Any recital, e.g. any statement of affection or other which you wish to pass
- A list of specific items to be left in your will
- A list of all pecuniary legacies, headed "I give and bequeath the following pecuniary legacies"

- A list of all gifts of land headed "I give and devise"
- A clause dealing with the residue of your estate, such as any property and money remaining after all the gifts and payments of expenses in your will have been made
- Your usual signature
- The signature of two witnesses, neither of whom or whose spouses are given any gift in the will. There should be a statement that they were both present at the same time and either saw you making your signature or acknowledging that the signature is yours.

Making a list of the key steps to be taken when preparing a will

It is essential, before beginning to draft out your will to follow a check list of the key steps to be taken:

- Make a complete list of all property that you own, including any future property. Deduct any mortgages or loans in order to arrive at a figure which can be left in your will, or a net worth
- Next, make a list of all those people who will benefit under your will (beneficiaries)
- Note any expressions of affection that you want to make in your will
- Organise your executors. As we have seen, these can be members of your family, a bank, solicitor etc. You need to know the fees involved if you are using a professional

practice. These should be allowed for in the will. Likewise, you may wish to leave something to those who act as executors for you

- Prepare your will, preferably typewritten on quality paper
- Make a list of all bequests of your goods that you wish to leave and a list of all the legacies of the money that you wish to leave
- Think about any specific beneficiaries and what this involves, such as a charity. Do you need to contact them and ask for their number or to enlist any help that they may give? Likewise, you may want to leave money to a pet. You will probably need advice on this
- Consider whether you want to create any trusts. Again, you will need advice concerning these
- Make sure that witnesses have signed your will
- Ensure that your signature is your usual one
- Make sure that the will is dated the day that it is signed.
- Fold up your will, place into an envelope and mark it "The last will and testament of_____ (add your name)
- Put your will in a safe place and tell your executors and next of kin where it is kept
- Remember to alter your will as your circumstances change. Destroy any old copies of wills.

The thirty-day clause

If your immediate beneficiary dies within days of your own demise, unlikely but not unknown, the situation may well arise where the gifts left by you will pass elsewhere. To prevent this happening, you can make provision in your will stipulating another beneficiary should the immediate beneficiary not survive you by thirty days.

The use of a statutory will form

Statutory will forms (which can be obtained from legal stationers) are very helpful in that they have the necessary forms of words, in many cases. There are a number of forms. Form 2 for example, allows you to give all your possessions to someone without having to identify each possession. There are a number of other forms catering for different situations. One such form is form 4 which is designed for charitable bequests.

International wills

A provision now exists which is designed to aid those people who have property in a number of different countries. They can now make one will and have it administered in any country which is party to the convention. This can be done regardless of where the will was drawn up or where the assets are. There are a certain number of criteria to be followed, however:

- The will must be in writing. It can be in any language
- The person whose will it is must declare in front of a solicitor/notary that the will is really his or hers and this must be witnessed by two people
- The person making the will must then sign it at the end, and sign and number each page, in the presence of a

solicitor and witnesses who must sign at the end. The date must be added, by a solicitor and a certificate must be attached, which should include details of where the will is kept.

It will be necessary to seek advice regarding international wills as they have only recently been introduced.

****

7

Intervention Of The Courts

Courts have wide powers to make alterations to a persons will, after that person's death. It can exercise these powers if the will fails to achieve the intentions of the person who wrote it, as a result of a clerical error or a failure to understand the instructions of the person producing the will. In addition, if mental illness can be demonstrated at the time of producing the will then this can also lead to the courts intervening.

In order to get the courts to exercise their powers, an application must be made within six months of the date on which probate is taken out. If gifts or other are distributed and a court order is made to rectify the will then all must be returned to be distributed in accordance with the court order. If any part of a persons will appears to have no meaning or is ambiguous then the court will look at any surrounding evidence and the testators intention and will rectify the will in the light of this evidence.

Right to dispose of property

In general, the law allows an unfettered right to dispose of a persons property as they choose. This however is subject to tax and the courts powers to intervene. The law has been consolidated in the Inheritance (Provision for Family and Dependants Act)

1975. Certain categories of people can now apply to the court and be given money out of a deceased person's will. This can be done whether there is a will or not.

The husband or wife of a deceased person can be given any amount of money as the court thinks reasonable. The 1975 Act implemented the recommendations of the Law Commission which felt that a surviving spouse should be given money out of an estate on the same principles as a spouse is given money when there is a divorce. This means that, even if a will is not made, or there are inadequate provisions then a surviving spouse can make an application to rectify the situation.

The situation is different for other relations. They can apply to the court to have a will rectified but will receive far less than the spouse. The following can claim against a will:

- The wife or husband of the deceased
- A former wife or former husband of the deceased who has not remarried
- A child of the deceased
- Any person who is not included as a child of the deceased but who was treated by the deceased as a child of the family in relation to any marriage during his lifetime
- Any other person who was being maintained, even if only partly maintained, by the deceased just before his or her death

Former spouse

There is one main condition under which a former spouse can claim and that is that they have not remarried. In addition, such a claim would be for only essential maintenance which would stop on remarriage. There is one key exception, that is that if your death occurs within a year of divorce or legal separation, your former spouse can make a claim.

Child of the deceased

As the above, any claim by children can only be on the basis of hardship.

Stepchildren

This includes anyone treated as your own child and supported by you, including illegitimate children or those conceived before, but not born till after, your death. The claim can only cover essential maintenance.

Dependants

This covers a wide range of potential claimants. Maintenance only is payable. There needs to be evidence of full or partial maintenance prior to death. Such support does not have to be financial, however.

There is another situation where the court can change a will after your death. This relates directly to conditions that you may have imposed on a beneficiary in order to receive a gift which are unreasonable. If the court decides that this is the case, that particular condition becomes void and does not have to be fulfilled.

If the condition involved something being done before the beneficiary receives the gift then the beneficiary does not receive the gift. If the condition involved something being done after the beneficiary received the gift then the beneficiary can have the gift without condition.

If the beneficiary does not receive the gift, as in the above, then either the will can make alternative provision or the gift can form part of the residue of the estate.

Unreasonable conditions can be many, one such being any condition that provides reason or incentive to break up a marriage, intention to remain celibate or not to remarry or one that separates children. There are others which impinge on religion, general behaviour and crime. An unreasonable condition very much depends on the perception of the beneficiary and the perception of the courts. A beneficiary can lose the right to a bequest, apart from any failure to meet conditions attached to a bequest. Again, a court will decide in what circumstance this is appropriate. Crime could be a reason, such as murder, or evidence of coercion or harassment of another person in pursuit of selfish gain.

8

Taxation

The formation of a will which enables you to minimise your tax liability is of the utmost importance. It is likely, if you are well off that you will want to consult a solicitor or financial advisor in order to gain the appropriate advice. It could be that you own a house which over the years has appreciated considerably which has resulted in the property being worth a considerable amount. This may mean that you could be liable for inheritance tax.

A book of this length cannot possibly give you in depth advice concerning your tax situation. However, what it can do is outline the current rules relating to tax and wills generally. It is very important to ensure that your will is updated regularly in order to keep abreast of the changing tax laws. The wealthier that you become the more important this becomes.

Deed of variation

Any change to a legal document is, in the main, achieved through a deed of variation. Within two years of a death, a beneficiary of a will may alter that deed in writing. For the purposes of inheritance tax the changed will is regarded as having been made by the dead person and substituted for that provision in the will or under the rules of intestacy. Tax will only be payable under the new provision. This is still true even if the beneficiary received the property and makes a gift of it or disclaims a legacy within two years of the death. The law governing this is set out in s. 142 Inheritance Tax Act 1984. In order to comply with s142 the disclaimer must be in writing, refer specifically to the provision in the will and be signed by the person making the change.

The deed should be sent as soon as possible to the Capital Taxes Office. Where a person redirects property or makes a gift of it within the two-year period he/she must give notice (written) to the Capital Taxes Office within six months of doing it that he wants this provision to apply. If the effect is to increase the liability to inheritance tax, then the executors must join in the notice and can refuse on the ground that they do not have sufficient assets in the estate to pay the extra tax.

Inheritance tax

Inheritance tax was introduced under the 1986 Finance Act to replace Capital Transfer Tax. It is a tax on what is known as "transfer of value" meaning transfer under the terms of a will, or the rules of intestacy which reduce an estate.

The amount which is liable to tax is the amount less any exemptions which are detailed further on. For tax purposes, the amount of the estate is the valuation of the estate of the dead person immediately before death. The tax is levied on transfers made by the dead person on death or *within seven years of death.*

Amount of inheritance tax payable

This is dependant on three factors:

- The value of the estate
- The value of any substantial gifts made within the last seven years
- Any exemptions from inheritance tax on ones death such as those on gifts to a surviving spouse, charities etc.

If a person is resident (domiciled) in the United Kingdom the tax applies to all that person property wherever it may be situated at home or abroad. If a person is domiciled abroad then the tax is applicable only to property in the United Kingdom.

The threshold for inheritance tax is 40% on the estate after exempt transfers and after the current tax threshold of £325,000 2009/10. The amount is increased (usually) each year from 6th April in line with the increase in the Retail Price Index for the year to the previous December. Inheritance tax is set at 20% on lifetime transfers.

Exemptions from tax

The following are exempt for the purposes of inheritance tax liability:

- All gifts between the dead person and spouse/civil partner. If the dead person is domiciled in the United Kingdom, and the husband/wife/civil partner is not then the exemption is limited to £55,000.

- Lifetime gifts which represent normal expenditure out of the dead persons income during their life. Where payments are made by the dead person which did not change the dead persons standard of living then such amounts if paid seven years prior to the death will not be included in the estate.

- Lifetime gifts not exceeding £3000 in any one tax year. A person can make gifts totaling not more than £3000 in any year irrespective of the number of people to whom the amounts are given, otherwise any amounts over this will be included in the value of the estate if the person dies within seven years.

- Gifts in any one tax year to a maximum of £250 per person. There is no limit on the number of people to whom such gifts can be given so long as each one does not exceed £250 in any one tax year. These amounts are additional to the £3000 mentioned above but only to the extent that the total to any one individual in any tax year does not exceed £250.

- Gifts in consideration of marriage. Wedding gifts by a parent to his or her child are exempt by up to £5000, by a grandparent or other more distant relative up to £2500 and by other people up to £1000. This applies to each parent or grandparent.

- Lifetime gifts for the maintenance of a spouse/civil partner or former spouse/civil partner, children and dependant relatives. In respect of a child, the exemption is to the age of 18 or completion of full time education if later. This is available for stepchildren and adopted children, plus illegitimate children. The child must be of the donor or his or her spouse.

- All gifts to charities
- Gifts to political parties unless they are made within the year of the date of the death, in which case up to £100,000 is exempt, but any amount above that will be included in the value of the estate.
- Gifts to organisations which deal with preservation of the national heritage or of a public nature such as the British Museum. This category includes gifts to most museums and art galleries.
- Certain types of properties are exempt, including agricultural land, business property, historic houses and woodlands plus works of art.

Married couples/civil partners and Inheritance tax
For the married couple/CP with a family who have acquired some wealth, the current state of the law provides a means of saving a significant amount of inheritance tax.

The use of the nil rate band
From the 9th of October 2007 it is possible for spouses and civil partners to transfer the nil rate band so that any part of the nil rate band that was not used when the first spouse or civil partner died

can be transferred to the individuals surviving spouse or civil partner for use after their death.

The family home

It often happens that the family home is owned jointly by husband and wife/civil partners and represents a large asset of the family. Property held by two or more people may be owned by them as joint tenants or tenants in common. Property owned by joint tenants passes automatically to the survivor on death but property owned by joint tenants does not. So if you and your spouse/civil partner own a property jointly, the survivor will own the property outright on death. On the other hand, if you own the family home as tenants in common then your share will pass according to what you say in your will.

Business property

Since 1992 there has been 100% relief for the following categories of business property:

- Sole proprietor or partner
- Life tenants business or interest in a business
- A holding of shares or securities which by itself, or in conjunction with other holdings owned by the transferor gives control of the company (whether quoted or unquoted)
- Unquoted shares which by themselves or in conjunction with other shares or securities owned by the transferor give control of more than 25% of the votes.

There is 50% relief for the following:

- Shares in a company which do not qualify under 3 above and which are not quoted on a recognised stock exchange.

- Land, buildings, plant or machinery owned by a partner or controlling shareholder and used wholly or mainly in the business of the partnership or company immediately before the transfer, provided that the partnership interest or shareholding would itself, if it were transferred, qualify for business relief.

- Any land or building, plant or machinery which, immediately before the transfer was used wholly for the purposes of a business carried on by the transferor, was settled property in which he or she was then beneficially entitled to an interest in possession and was transferred while the business itself was being retained.

Potentially Exempt Transfers

Any gift outside the exemptions mentioned above which is made within seven years of the persons death will be included in the value of the estate. Any gift made more than seven years from the death of the person making it is free of any liability for tax. These gifts are known as "Potentially Exempt Transfers" (PETS) and become wholly exempt once seven years have elapsed and the donor is still alive. If the donor dies within seven years of making the gift only a percentage of the tax payable will be due, depending on how long before the death it was made, in keeping with the following scale:

6-7 years   20% of gift at rate of 8%
5-6 years   40% of gift at rate of 16%
4-5 years   60% of gift at rate of 24%
3-4 years   80% of gift at rate of 32%
up to 3 years 100% of gift at rate of 40%

Free standing income tax charge

In his budget of March 2004, the Chancellor of the Exchequer outlined proposals for a 'free standing income tax charge', based on 'pre-owned assets. This is, in part, a device which helps the treasury overcome various schemes to avoid the payment of tax. This income tax charge came into force on 6th April 2005 and applies to both tangible and intangible assets and to any funds or contributions to the funds used to acquire the assets whether the funds or contributions are directly or indirectly provided.

The income tax charge is similar to the income tax charge made upon employees for benefits in kind supplied by their employers and quantifies in cash the annual benefit enjoyed. It is equivalent in the case of property to the annual rental value of the asset or in the case of other assets, the value of the asset at a rate of interest, and in each case less any payment made under a legally binding agreement for the use of the asset.

After the deduction of the amount paid for the benefit, the sum so ascertained is added to your taxable income and taxed at your top rate of tax. The first £5,000 per annum is ignored but once the

£5000 exemption is exceeded, the exemption is totally lost. The income tax charge does not apply to the extent that:

- The asset was disposed of before 18th March 1986
- The original gift was for the maintenance of your family or within the small gifts exemption or within the inheritance tax annual gifts allowance.
- The formerly owned asset is currently owned by your spouse or civil partner
- The asset still counts as an asset for inheritance tax purposes under the gift with a reservation rules
- The asset was transferred to your spouse, former spouse, civil partner or former civil partner by court order
- In the case of an outright gift of money made more than seven years or more before the earliest date before which you either occupied the land or had the use of the land as applicable
- The asset was sold for cash at arms length whether or not the parties were connected persons
- The owner of the asset was formerly the owner of the asset only by virtue of a will or intestacy which has subsequently been varied by agreement between the parties (i.e. by deed of family arrangement)
- Any enjoyment is no more than incidental, including cases where an out and out gift to a family member comes to benefit the giver as a result of a change in their circumstances.

Neither does the income tax charge apply if the total tax payable in the relevant tax year does not exceed £5000 but if it does the benefit of the exemption is lost and tax is payable on the entire sum, not just on the excess.

Former owners are not regarded as enjoying a taxable benefit if they retain an interest which is consistent with their ongoing enjoyment of the property.

If you elect on or before 31st January in the year of assessment immediately following upon the first year of assessment in which the charge applies to the property concerned you may choose to have the property concerned treated as part of your estate for inheritance tax purposes as a gift with reservation of an interest rather than have the benefit taxed as income. In those circumstances, the property will be eligible for the normal IHT relief and exemptions available,

Only assets in the UK are affected by the scheme imposing the income tax liability in respect of pre-owned assets if you do not have and are not deemed to have a U.K. domicile. If you do it applies in respect of all your assets, wherever the assets are.

If you give an asset away and pay a full commercial rent or hiring fee to use it, although doing so will save inheritance tax, it will not be an otherwise tax efficient transaction because, as far as income tax is concerned, you will be paying the rent out of your taxed income and the recipient of the gift will have to pay income tax on the rest.

Moreover, if it was your principal private residence you will lose your capital gains tax exemptions for a principal private residence.

Life Insurance Policies

If a person has a life insurance policy on his or her life and for own benefit the value of the policy forms part of the estate. If there is a gift of the policy during that persons lifetime then the premium payment and not the policy becomes a potentially exempt transfer which will not be included in that persons estate if they survive seven years after the gift. If a policy is taken out for the benefit of another person it is the premium payment which is the PET and not the value of the policy.

Policies such as this can be a useful way of making provision for inheritance tax liability on an estate as a whole.

Gifts with reservation

One way in which a person may seek to minimise inheritance tax liability is to reduce the value of the estate by making gifts before death. As demonstrated, these will be regarded as PETS and may be brought into the estate if death occurs within seven years. There is another factor to be considered. If a person gives something away but still continues to enjoy it or derive a benefit from it, then such a gift will form part of the estate whenever it was made so long as the donor continued to enjoy it up to his or her death. This is known as a "gift with reservation" because the donor reserves a benefit. To avoid a gift with reservation, the gift must be enjoyed by the person to whom it has been given.

The payment of tax

Whenever money is left in a will consideration needs to be given as to whether inheritance tax attributable to it is to be paid out of the residue of the estate or to be paid by the person receiving the legacy. If inheritance tax comes from the residue of the estate then it should be declared to be free of tax, if paid by the person to whom it is left, it is declared subject to tax.

Deductions from the estate

From the overall value of the estate for inheritance tax purposes, reasonable funeral expenses can be deducted. In addition, any additional expenses incurred in administering or realising property outside of the United Kingdom against its value (to a maximum of 50%) can be realised.

Gifts to charitable institutions

Gifts to charities are exempt at any time whether as lifetime gifts or passed under the terms of a will. They can be expressed as either to a specific charity or as an amount to be distributed by the dead persons trustees. These can be the same as the executors in which case they should be named as trustees as well as executors.

In many cases a person will make a will many years before death. This could mean that unless a will is revised regularly, the amounts of money specified as bequests may become devalued through inflation so that on death they no longer represent the original size of the gift that was intended.

One common way of overcoming this is to express the gift as a percentage or proportion of the overall net estate.

If you wish a bequest to go to a specific branch of a charity this must be specified, otherwise the gift will go to head office as a matter of course.

9

Making a Will in Scotland

There are a number of key differences for a will made in Scotland, which need to be highlighted:

- Intestacy

If you do not make a will in Scotland before you die, the law is a s follows:

- If there is a spouse/civil partner but no other close family, such as children, parents, brothers and sisters etc, then the spouse benefits from the whole estate.
- If there is a spouse/civil partner and there are children, then the spouse can have property (or £50,000 if it is worth more) furniture and personal possessions up to a value of £10,000, cash up to £15,000 and a third of the remainder of the state (excluding other property). Children (or their children) share what is left in equal proportion.
- If there is no spouse/civil partner but there are children then they or their children benefit from the estate in equal shares. (not stepchildren).
- If there is no spouse or children, but there are parents, brothers and sisters then the parents take half of the estate and the other half is divided equally between any brothers

and sisters or their children. Where only one of these groups is alive, those concerned benefit from the whole estate.

If none of the above applies, then the following benefit, in this order:

- Full uncles/aunts or their children
- Half uncles/aunts or their children
- Grandparents
- Full great uncles/aunts (or descendants)
- Half great uncles/aunts (or descendants)
- Great grandparents

If no relatives can be found then the Crown takes the estate and can distribute it among anyone with a reasonable claim.

- **Age**

Whereas in the rest of the United Kingdom you need to be over 18 to make a will, in Scotland the age limit is lower. For a male it is over fourteen and twelve for a female.

- **Marriage**

In Scotland, marriage does not revoke a will.

- **Children**

Elsewhere in the United Kingdom this applies to illegitimate and adopted children, in Scotland you have to specify their status in the will. If you have children after making a will and have not made any mention of them the will is considered null and void. A new will needs to be produced.

- **Presentation**

If you produce the whole of your will by hand, then you do not need any witnesses. You must sign at the bottom of every page, not just the last page. If the will is not completely handwritten then you will need two witnesses.

- **Claims against your estate**

In Scotland, the spouse and children have more rights to claim against the estate than the rest of the United Kingdom, even if there is provision in the will to specifically exclude them. The law equally applies against any claims from others who were partly or totally dependent on the dead person before death.

SECTION 2-
ADMINISTERING ESTATES

10

Administering An Estate

The formalities

Relatives or friends of the deceased will take on the task of dealing with the necessary formalities after death. In the first instance, notwithstanding where the person dies, a doctor must provide relatives with a certificate stating the cause of death. This certificate is then lodged at the Registry of Births Deaths and Marriages within five days of the issue. The registrar will need to know full details of the death and will also ask for any other certificates such as marriage and birth. The person who registers the death is known as the 'informant'.

If the doctor states that the cause of death is uncertain, then the arrangements are rather more complex. The death will first be reported to the coroner, who usually orders a post-mortem. If it shows that the cause of death was natural, the coroner then authorises the burial or cremation. In these cases, you will be issued with a death certificate by the Registrar and a second certificate permitting the undertaker to arrange burial or cremation.

Except in rare cases, for example violent death when the coroner orders an inquest to be held, it will now be time to organise the funeral. It will be necessary at this point to check the will or if there is no will, to find out about the arrangements for administering the estate.

Funeral arrangements

If there is a will in existence, it may well contain details concerning the desired funeral arrangements of the deceased. If there are no clear instructions the executors of the will usually make appropriate arrangements. The executor will become legally liable to pay costs of the funeral.

Where the deceased dies intestate, the 'administrators' of the estate will instruct the undertaker and assume responsibility for payments. In some cases, it may be clear that the deceased does not have enough assets to cover the funeral. If this is the case then investigations need to take place, including the possibility of a one-off funeral grant to cover costs. Once financial details have been settled it is advisable to put a notice in the deaths column of one or more papers to bring the funeral to the attention of relatives.

The responsibilities of executors

Executors and administrators of estates have very important responsibilities. In the first instance they are responsible for ensuring that the assets of the estate are paid to the correct beneficiaries of the will and also for ensuring that all debts are paid before distribution. If this aspect of administration is mismanaged then the executor or administrator will be held, or could be held, liable for any debts. In order to ensure that they are protected then executors or administrators should advertise in the London gazette – which is a newspaper for formal notices of any kind, and also a local paper together with requests that creditors should submit their claims by a date which must be at least two months after the advertisement. Private individuals will usually have to produce a copy of probate before their advertisement is accepted for publication.

The executor's initial steps

If you are the executor of a valid will (or if you are the administrator if there is no will) you can now begin the task of administering the estate. It will be essential to ensure that the basic elements are dealt with such as informing utilities, arranging for termination of certain insurance policies and discharge of liabilities of others such as life insurance. Arrangements will need to be made for any pets and post redirected. These are the basic essential lifestyle elements before you make an application for probate.

The value of the estate

Before you can apply for probate of the will, you have to find out the extent and value of the assets and liabilities of the estate. You will need to have access to all records of assets, such as insurance policies and bank accounts. The ease with which you can establish a total value will depend on how organised the deceased was. If the deceased was a taxpayer it is advisable to approach the local tax office for a copy of his or her last tax return, sending a copy of the will to prove your status as an executor.

Once you have collated all proof of assets including property you will need to arrive at a total value. The following will provide a pointer for establishing value:

Bank accounts
Interest-bearing accounts and joint bank accounts
When you have found out details of these accounts you should ask for details of balance and accrued interest at the time of death. This is needed for the tax return you will have to complete on behalf of the deceased estate.

These types of accounts can be problematic. If the joint holders are husband and wife, the account will pass automatically to the survivor. In other cases you will need to establish the intentions of the joint owners or the contribution of each to the joint account. This is because the amount contributed by the deceased forms part of the estate for tax purposes (except where a written agreement confirms that the money in the account passes automatically to the survivor). In the case of business partnership accounts, you need a set of final trading accounts to the date of death and should contact the surviving partner.

National Savings
These may take the form of National Savings Certificates, National Savings Investment Accounts or Premium Bonds. A

claim form for repayment should be obtained, usually from the post office and sent to the appropriate department for National Savings together with a copy of the probate when you have it.

Building societies
You would approach a building society in the same way as a bank, asking for a balance and interest to date. You should also ask for a claim form for payment.

Life insurance
You should write to insurance companies stating the date of death and the policy number and enclose a copy of the death certificate. Once probate has been obtained submit your claim form for monies owed. In many cases, policies are held on trust and will not form part of an estate. Insurance companies will, on production of the death certificate, make payment direct to the beneficiaries.

Stock and shares
You should make arrangements to forward a list of stocks and shares held by the deceased to a bank or stockbroker. In the case of Pep's and ISA's you should send them to the plan manger and ask for a valuation. Ask for transfer forms for all shareholdings.

You may decide to value the stocks and shares yourself. If this is the case, you will need a copy of the official Stock Exchange Daily Official List for the day on which the deceased died. The valuation figure is calculated by adding 25% of the difference between the selling and buying prices. If the death took place at the weekend you can choose either the Monday or Friday Valuation.

However, if the executors sell any shares at a loss within 12 months, the selling price in all cases can be taken as the value at the date of death.

If you cannot locate all of the share certificates, you may be able to find dividend counterfoils or tax vouchers among the papers of the deceased which will enable you to check the number of shares held in the company. If you cannot find share certificates, write to the Registrar of the company. Name of Registrars are given in the Register of Registrars held in the local library. The same approach can be made if the deceased holds unit trusts. In the case of private companies where no value of shares is published, you may sometimes be able to obtain a valuation from the secretary of the company. In the case of a family company it will usually be necessary to have the value determined by a private accountant.

Pensions

If the deceased was already receiving a pension, you should write to the company operating the scheme in order to find out further details, i.e. is the pension paid up until the time of death, are there any other beneficiaries after death and so on. Pensions vary significantly and it is very important that accurate information is obtained.

State benefits

If the deceased was in receipt of an old age pension, notice of the death should be given to the Department of Work and Pensions, so that any adjustments can be made. In the case of married men, the agency will make arrangements to begin to pay widows pension.

Businesses

The valuation of a business on the death of one of the partners is complicated and depends upon the nature of the business, the way in which the accounts are prepared and the extent of the assets held by the business. The surviving partner/s should make available a set of partnership accounts to the date of death and help you to determine the correct valuation for the deceased share.

Farms

If the deceased had an interest in a farm, any type of farm you should seek advice of a more specialist agricultural valuer.

Residential property

If the estate is below the inheritance tax threshold, you may be able to estimate the value of the property by looking at similar properties in estate agents windows. You may also wish to obtain a professional valuation. If the estate reaches the inheritance tax threshold or is close to it, the figure is checked by the District Valuer. If the property is sold within four years of death for less than the probate valuation, and providing the sellers are executors and not beneficiaries, the sale price may be substituted for the original valuation.

In the case of joint properties, the value of the person who has died forms part of the estate for tax purposes. However, if the share passes to the spouse, the 'surviving spouse exemption' applies. This means that there is no inheritance tax to pay, even if the estate exceeds the inheritance tax threshold.

If there is a mortgage on the property at the date of death, the amount of the debt must be found by writing to the bank or building society. The value of the house is reduced by this amount.

Where the deceased has left residential property as a specific item, the will may either say that the property is to be transferred to the beneficiary free from any mortgage or that it is subject to a mortgage, The Administration of Estates Act provides that a person who is bequeathed a mortgaged property is responsible for repaying the mortgage unless the will sets out a contrary intention.

Other property and buildings

If the deceased owned commercial property, the executor has to determine whether this was a business asset or whether it is an investment property unconnected with any business. If this is the case a separate valuation will be needed.

Personal possessions

Although it is not always necessary to obtain professional valuations for household goods, estimated values are examined very carefully by the District Valuer if the estate is large enough to attract inheritance tax. The way household goods are dealt with will depend entirely on their value. In certain cases, with items such as painting and jewellery then an auction may be appropriate.

Income tax

It is very unlikely that, before you make your application for probate, you will be in a position to calculate the income tax owed on an estate. As the administration of the estate gathers momentum then you will amass enough information to start forming a picture of the value and thus the tax liabilities.

11

Probate

Applying for probate

Probate represents the official proof the validity of a will and is granted by the court on production by the executors of the estate of the necessary documents. Only when probate is obtained are executors free to administer and distribute the estate.

If the value of the estate is under £5000 in total, it may be possible to administer the estate without obtaining probate. Generally, if the estate is worth more than £5000, you will have to apply for probate of the will or letters of administration. There are a number of reasons for this:

- Banks, building societies and National Savings are governed by the Administration of Estates (Small payments) Act 1965. This only allows them to refund individual accounts up to £5000 without production of probate.
- You cannot sell stocks, shares or land from an estate without probate, except in the case of land held in names of joint tenants where this passes on after death
- If the administration is disputed or if a person intends to make a claim as a dependant or member of the family, his or her claim is 'statute barred' six months after the grant of

probate. The right to take action remains open if the estate is administered without probate

- A lay executor who managed to call in the assets of an estate without probate might miss the obligation to report matters to the Inland Revenue for inheritance tax purposes, especially where a substantial gift had been made in the seven years prior to the death.

Letters of administration

If someone dies intestate (without making a will) the rules of intestacy laid down by Act of Parliament will apply. An administrator must apply for letters of administration for exactly the same reasons as the executor applies for probate. The grant of letters of administration will be made to the first applicant.

If a will deals with part only but not all of the administration (for example where the will defines who receives what but does not name an executor) the person entitled to apply for letters of administration make the application to the Registrar attaching the will at the same time. The applicant is granted 'Letters of administration with will attached'.

Applying for letters of administration

The following demonstrates the order of those entitled to apply:

- The surviving spouse (not unmarried partner)
- The children or their descendants (once over 18)

You do not have to sign form PA1. At the end of the process, the probate registry will couch the information you supply in legal jargon for the document you are required to sign.

Form PA1 contains a reminder that you have to attach the death certificate, the will and the completed form 1HT 205. If this form demonstrates that the estate exceeds the 'excepted estate' threshold (for inheritance tax purposes) form 1HT 200 will have to be completed.

Sending the forms

If the estate you are administering can be contained on form 1HT 205, you are ready to send in your application. Make sure that you take photocopies of all material. You should send the following:

- The will

- The death certificate

- Probate application form PA1

- Short form 1HT 205

- A cheque for the fee and copies

Attach any explanatory letter as necessary. You should then send the package by registered post. A few weeks later, you will be invited to review the documents, pay the probate fee and swear the prescribed oath. Remember to take your file of background papers.

Probate fees are calculated on the amount of the net estate, as declared for the purpose of inheritance tax. Fees are payable when you attend the interview at the registry – see form PA4 for guidance.

Attendance at the probate registry

When you arrive at the probate registry you will need to examine the forms that have been prepared for you. You need to satisfy yourself that all the details are correct. When you have checked all the details, the commissioner will ask you to sign the original will and swear the oath, identifying the will as that of the deceased.

The actual process entails you standing up, holding a copy of the New Testament and repeating the words spoken by the commissioner. The words take the form of 'I swear by Almighty God that this is my name and handwriting and that the contents of this my oath are true and that this is the will referred to'. The form of oath is varied depending on religious belief or otherwise. The commissioner will then sign beneath your signature on the official form and will. The fees are paid and any sealed copies as ordered will be supplied.

Letters of administration

If the deceased has left no will, then the next of kin will apply for a grant of letters of administration instead of probate. The same is the case if a will was left but no executors appointed. In these cases, the grant is called letters of administration with will annexed'

When letters of administration are sought, the administrators may in some cases have to provide a guarantee – for example where the beneficiaries are under age or mentally disabled or when the administrator is out of the country. The guarantee is provided by an insurance company at a cost or by individuals who undertake to make good – up to the gross value of the estate – any deficiency caused by the administrators failing in their duties.

Letters of administration may also be taken out by creditors of an estate if executors deliberately do not apply for probate – for instance, if the estate has insufficient assets to pay all creditors and legatees.

Inheritance tax and form 1HT 200

Form 1HT 200 is the Inland Revenue account for inheritance tax. It should be completed by reference to form 1HT 210, guidance notes. 1HT consists of eight pages. Take time and care with this form. It is relatively uncomplicated.

The grant of probate

There may be a time lapse of six weeks or more between lodging the probate papers and the meeting at the registry to sign and swear them. After this has happened, however, things move quickly. If there is no inheritance tax to be paid – where the net estate is less than £325,000 (2009/10) or where the deceased property goes to the spouse – the grant of probate (or letters of administration) is issued within a few days. If inheritance tax is due, it takes two to three weeks before the exact amount is calculated and the grant is usually ready about a week later.

The grant of probate is signed by an officer of the probate registry. Attached to the grant of probate is a photocopy of the will. (all original wills are kept at the Principal Probate Registry in London). Each page of your copy of the will carries the impress of the courts official seal. It is accompanied by a note which explains the procedure for collecting and distributing the estate and advises representatives to take legal advice in the event of dispute or other difficulty.

12

Distribution of an Estate

The distribution of the estate of the deceased

Having established probate, it is now time to begin to distribute the estate. Before you can do this, however, it is essential that you understand exactly what the will says. The executor can be sued for payment if the estate is not distributed exactly in accordance with the stipulations in the will. Although this may sound like common sense, some wills may be couched in a particular way, or in a particular jargon and you may need advice on the interpretation.

Specific legacies and bequests

Legacies are, usually, the payment of specific sums of money. Bequests usually mean gifts of goods or cash. 'Devises' means gifts of land or buildings. If the state is not subject to inheritance tax and the legacies and bequests are small, legacies can be paid without further delay and also specific items can be handed over. It is advisable to obtain a receipt from the beneficiary(s) when they receive their gift or legacy.

One common problem that can arise is trying to trace beneficiaries. This is usually done through the local or national press if the beneficiary is not forthcoming.

Transferring property

If a beneficiary has been left a house or other property then any outstanding debts relating to the property, such as a mortgage have to be dealt with. The will usually directs the executors to pay off the mortgage. However, if the will is silent on this point then it will become the responsibility of the beneficiary. It is quite usual that a property is left to another with a mortgage and equity in the property so the beneficiary can continue to pay.

It will be necessary to transfer the property into your own name by contacting the Land Registry. If the property is already registered, as is most property, the process will be straightforward. However, if it is unregistered then you will need to obtain a first registration. You would probably need to instruct a solicitor to do this. At the same time obtain advice about settling the mortgage.

Preparation of final accounts

Having gathered the assets and obtained a good idea of the value you can now begin to prepare final accounts. There is no set form for the final accounts but assets and liabilities must be included, receipts and payments made during the administration and a distribution account of payments to beneficiaries.

It is helpful to include a covering sheet to the accounts, a form of memorandum which will cover the following areas:

- Details of the deceased and date of death, date of probate and names of executors
- A summary of the bequests made in the will

- Particulars of property transfers
- Reference to any valuations which have been included in the accounts

In estates where inheritance tax has been paid, you should prepare one part of the capital account based on the value of the assets at the time of death.

The second part of the account should demonstrate the value of those assets and liabilities at the date they are realised or paid. If the net effect is to reduce the value of the estate, you may be able to claim a refund from the capital taxes office. Conversely you may have increased taxes to pay. In either case you should advise the capital taxes office.

A model set of accounts are shown in the appendix. The capital account shows the value of assets when they are cashed or realised and the debts are the sums actually paid. The income account shows the income received during the administration, less associated expenses. It is convenient to run this account from the date of death to the following 5th of April.

The distribution account shows the capital and income transferred from the respective accounts and how the residue of the estate has been divided. If there is only one beneficiary you should show the final figure. If any items have been taken in kind – such as a car or a piece of furniture – its value is included in the distribution account as both an asset and payment. If you are claiming executor's expenses itemise them and include them in the distribution account.

Where a will exists

When you have completed your accounts, and all outstanding debts and liabilities have been met, you will now be in a position to calculate how much each residuary beneficiary receives according to the specific provisions of the will. In practice, the amount that you have left in the executor's bank account should match the sums to be paid out.

After having ascertained that this is the case, and rectified any errors you should send the accounts to the beneficiaries for their agreement or otherwise. In cases involving inheritance tax, you should contact the capital taxes office and confirm that you have disclosed the full value of the estate. You then apply for a clearance certificate. When you have received this you can make the final distribution to the beneficiaries. The beneficiaries should be asked to sign an acknowledgement that they agree the accounts and that they agree the amount that they will receive.

Where beneficiaries are deceased or missing

If a beneficiary dies before the death of the testator, the general rule is that the legacy cannot be made. There are a few exceptions to this rule:

- If the will contains a 'substitution' (an alternative to the beneficiary)

- If the gift is made to two people as joint tenants – the survivor being the beneficiary
- If section 33(2) of the Wills Act 1837 applies. This section provides that, if the share of the estate or gift is to a child or other descendant of the testator and the child dies before the testator leaving 'issue' (children and their descendants) they take the share of the gift.

If a beneficiary cannot be located, you must take steps to find that person. These steps must be reasonable. As stated, an advertisement can suffice, as well as contacting relatives and so on. You can apply to the court for an order giving you permission to distribute the estate on agreed terms You can claim any expenses incurred from the estate.

It is very important, if you cannot find a beneficiary that you take steps to obtain a court order in order to protect yourself from any future problems arising should a beneficiary turn up.

The children's trust under intestacy rules

We saw earlier in the book how an estate is distributed according to the rules of intestacy. When the surviving spouse has children, whatever their age, and the estate is worth more than £125,000, the administrators of the estate must set up a trust to look after the children's share. As trustees, they must invest half the remaining capital in their own names. They notify the Inland Revenue of the new trust and submit a Trust Tax return each year. The income from the trust is paid to the spouse. On the death of the spouse, the capital held in the trust account is shared between the children unless they are under 18.

If any of the children die, leaving children of their own, before the death of the intestate or – whichever is the later – second parent, the Statutory Trust rules apply. Under these rules, where a child of the intestate has died leaving children who are 18 or over (or who marry before 18) the children get their parents share. The same applies if the only survivors are grandchildren or even remote descendants.

In some cases, intestacy rules can be rigid and cause hardship. You should always take advice when dealing with distribution of assets in cases that are complicated to resolve.

13

Administering Estates in Scotland

There are significant differences between the law of England and Wales and the law of Scotland.

Personal representatives in Scotland

In Scotland, all personal representatives are known as executors. The title of 'administrator' is unknown. An executor appointed by a will is called an 'executor-nominate' and the executor of an estate of a person who has died without making a valid will or who has left no will at all is known as an 'executor dative'. Scottish law prescribes an order of applicants for the position of executor-dative. This applicant is usually a close member of the deceased's family. The application for appointment as executor-dative is normally handled by a solicitor.

In contrast to the position in England and Wales, the appointment of all executors, generally speaking, must be confirmed by the Scottish courts before the executor can begin to deal with the administration of the deceased's estate.

If an executor nominate does not wish to act, he cannot be compelled to do so. If the deceased appointed other executors by his will, those who are willing to act may apply for their appointment to be confirmed, the renouncing executor being required to sign a statement that he does not wish to act.

How Scottish law regards property

In Scottish law, property may be classified as heritable or moveable. Heritable property includes land and buildings, moveable property includes money, personal possessions, investments and bank and building society accounts. Both types of property may be owned by one person or more. Property owned by two or more persons may be held by them jointly or in common. It is more usual for property to be held in common. Heritable property held in common by the deceased and others forms part of the deceased's estate to the extent of his interest in it. Such property passes under the will or in accordance with the intestacy rules unless the deeds contain a statement – known as a 'survivorship destination' – that is to pass to the survivor of the co-owners.

The same cannot be said for moveable property. It is common for bank or building society accounts of married couples to be maintained as common property and operated on the basis that either of them can sign cheques during their lifetimes and that on first death the survivor can continue to operate the account. This relationship does not regulate the ownership of the money in the account, which belongs to the account holder in the proportions in which they contributed, unless there is an intention to combine resources.

Confirmation

The general rule is that confirmation is needed in all but the following cases:

1) The property in the deceased's estate has been nominated. The rules are broadly the same as those in England and Wales

2) The only payments to be made to beneficiaries are small, currently not exceeding £5,000.

3) The property owned by the deceased was held in common with others and there is a valid survivorship destination, In these circumstances, the deceased's interest passes directly to the survivor.

Estates of £25,000 or less

If the gross value of the deceased's estate is £25.000 or less, there is a special procedure for obtaining confirmation. There is no need to petition the court for the appointment of an executor and the court will complete the necessary forms.

No will

If a deceased made no will or made a will that is not valid, the court must appoint an executor, usually someone who is entitled to inherit. The intending executor must draw up a list of assets and liabilities stating their values and send it to court where the information will be recorded on an official form (C1). The applicant will then be asked to attend court together with two witnesses who can assure the court that the applicant is who he says he is and who can verify his relationship to the deceased.

At this stage, the applicant will usually need to satisfy the court that he will be able to carry out his duties. This is done by obtaining a bond from an insurance company or sometimes from an individual of good standing for an amount equivalent to the gross value of the estate. This is known as a 'bond of caution'. Sometimes insurance companies will refuse to issue bonds of cautions to executors who wish to act for themselves. In these circumstances, the executors have no choice but to instruct solicitors to act on their behalf unless they can find a person of suitable financial standing.

Will

The procedure is similar to that outlined above, except that:

1) The applicant must send the original will to the court at the same time as the list of assets and liabilities. The will should then be returned when confirmation is issued.
2) No bond of caution is required.
3) There is no need for independent witnesses to attend court when form C1 is signed.

In contrast to England and Wales, in Scotland there are no special procedures or forms used by personal representatives who wish to act personally without professional assistance. Nor is any special provision made by the court to help such persons. The following steps need to be taken:

1) Complete the appropriate application form(s). these can be obtained from the Capital Taxes Office, HM Commissary office, Sheriff Court and main post offices. Alternatively they can be downloaded from the internet (www.inlandrevenue.gov/uk/cto).

2) Form C1. This is the form required to enable you to act as executor of the deceased's estate. It must be completed whenever confirmation is required.

3) Form IHT200. If the inventory contained within form C1 shows that the gross value of the deceased's estate exceeds £220,000 you will need to complete form IHT200. This form may also have to be completed even if the gross value is less than the figure if certain other conditions are not satisfied. The guidance notes to form C1 explain this.

Having completed form C1, you must sign the declaration on page 2.

Where inheritance tax is payable

If you completed form IHT200, it is likely that inheritance tax is payable. You should send the following documents to the Capital Taxes Office. The Capital taxes Office will check your calculations and then send you a receipt to show that all tax due has now been paid. You will need to send this to the Sheriffs Court. The inheritance tax payable at this stage is a provisional amount and further tax may be payable or a refund made depending on the value of the assets in the deceased's estate. You should send a cheque for inheritance tax to HMRC.

The final step in the process

The last step is to file the documents required for confirmation. These consist of:

- The Capital Taxes Offices's receipt for inheritance tax.
- The will (and supporting documentation).
- A cheque for the prescribed amount.

All these documents should be sent or handed in to the appropriate Sheriffs Court. This is the court for the place of the deceased's residence at his death. If the court has a query it will contact you. Otherwise it will issue the confirmation and return the will, usually within 10-14 days of lodgement.

Executors powers and duties

For most practical purposes these are broadly in line with those of executors in England and Wales.

Administering and distributing the estate

Once the confirmation has been issued, you can administer and distribute the estate in accordance with the will or intestacy rules. There are several key differences between the position of an executor of an English or Welsh estate and a Scottish estate, including the following.

Unknown creditors

There is no provision under Scottish law that corresponds directly to the Trustee act 1925, section 27. Instead, executors have the right to pay all known creditors and to distribute the deceased's estate to those beneficially entitled after six months have elapsed from the date of death. Any creditor who submits a late claim stands to lose his money if the estate has been distributed unless it can be proved that the executors should have known of the creditors existence. Notwithstanding this protection, if there is any doubt in your mind about the nature and extent of the deceased's creditors, it is sensible to advertise the death in a newspaper circulating in the area where the deceased lived.

Debts

After all the assets have been collected in, it is essential that all known debts are settled before any amount is paid to the beneficiaries. Debts of an insolvent estate must be paid in the following order:

- Deathbed and reasonable funeral expenses
- Secured debts, for example, a mortgage
- Preferred debts, for example taxes and national insurance contributions
- Ordinary debts

Each category of debts must be paid in full before the next category. Within each category, each creditor is paid the same proportion if all the creditors cannot be paid in full. When all the debts have been paid, you can distribute the estate to those beneficially entitled. Gifts of land are made by a document called a 'docket' unless the title deeds contain a survivorship destination to a beneficiary under the will or under the intestacy rules or who has prior legal rights. Sales, as distinct from gifts, are made by a document called a 'disposition'.

Insolvent estates

The position of a Scottish executor is broadly the same as an executor in the estate of England and Wales. If the estate is or appears to be insolvent you should seek legal advice straightaway.

Glossary of terms

Administrator
The person who administers the estate of a person who has died intestate

Bequest
A gift of a particular object or cash as opposed to 'devise' which means land or buildings

Chattels
Personal belongings of the deceased

Child
Referred to in a will or intestacy – child of the deceased including adopted and illegitimate children but, unless specifically included in a will, not stepchildren

Cohabitee
A partner of the deceased who may be able to claim a share of the estate. The term 'common law wife' has no legal force.

Confirmation
The document issued to executors by the sheriff court in Scotland to authorise them to administer the estate

Devise
A gift of house or land

Disposition
A formal conveyancing document in Scotland

Estate
Al the assets and property of the deceased, including houses, cars, investments, money and personal belongings

Executor
The person appointed in the will to administer the estate of a deceased person

Heritable estate
Land and buildings in Scotland

Inheritance tax
The tax which may be payable when the total estate of the deceased person exceeds a set threshold (subject to various exemptions and adjustments)

Intestate
A person who dies without making a will

Issue
Al the descendants of a person, i.e. children, grandchildren, great grandchildren#

Legacy
A gift of money

Minor
A person under 18 years of age

Moveable estate
Property other than land or buildings in Scotland

Next of Kin
The person entitled to the estate when a person dies intestate

Letters of administration
The document issued to administrators by a probate registry to authorise them to administer the estate of an intestate

Personal estate or personalty
Al the investments and belongings of a person apart from land and buildings

Personal representatives
A general term for both administrators and executors

Probate of the will
The document issued to executors by a probate registry in England, Wales and Northern Ireland to authorise them to administer the estate

Probate Registry
The Government office which deals with probate maters. The principal Probate Registry is in London with district registries in cities and some large towns

Real estate or realty
Land and buildings owned by a person

Residue
What is left of the estate to share out after all the debts and specific bequests and legacies have been paid

Specific bequests
Particular items gifted by will

Testator
A person who makes a will

Will
The document in which you say what is to happen to your estate after death

Useful Addresses

Department for National Savings
Glasgow G58 1SB
For enquiries about Capital Bonds, Children's Bonus Bonds,
FIRST Option Bonds, Fixed Rate Savings Bonds, Ordinary
Accounts and Investment Accounts.

Department for National Savings
Durham DH99 1NS
Enquiries about deposit bonds, Cash mini-ISA's Savings
Certificates, SAYE Contracts and Yearly Plan Agreements

Department for National Savings
Blackpool FY3 9YP
Enquiries about Premium Bonds, Pensioners guaranteed bonds

Tel 0845 964 5000 (Central Helpline)
www.nationalsavings.co.uk

Department of Work and Pensions
Newcastle Benefits Directorate
Longbenton
Newcastle Upon Tyne NE98 1zz
For pensions enquiries
0191 213 5000
www.dss.gov.uk

Inland Revenue Capital Taxes Office
Ferrers House
PO Box 38
Castle Meadow Road
Nottingham NG2 1BB
0115 974 2400
www.inlandrevenue.gov.org

The Law Society of England and Wales
113 Chancery lane
London WC2A 1PL
0870 606 6575
Public information including solicitors who specialise in wills and probate
www.lawsociety.org.uk

London Gazette
PO Box 7923
London SE1 5ZH
020 7394 4580

Office for the Supervision of Solicitors
Victoria Court
8 Dormer Place
Leamington Spa
Warwickshire CV32 5AE
0845 608 6565

www.solicitors-online.com
Information on solicitors specialising in wills and probate

The Principal Probate Registry

First Avenue House
42-49 High Holborn
London WC1V 6NP

020 7947 6939 (Information and adv ice)
020 7947 7602 (For the hard of hearing)
020 7947 6983 (Orderline for probate forms and guidance notes)
www.courtservice.gov.uk

OYEZ Straker

Oyez House
16 Third Avenue
Denbigh West Industrial Estate
Bletchley
Milton Keynes MK1 1TG

01908 361166
Tele sales for probate forms and other stationary.

Useful Addresses in Scotland
Accountant of Court

2 Parliament Square
Edinburgh EH1 1RQ

0131 240 6758

www.scotscourts.gov.uk

Inland Revenue Capital Taxes
Meldrum House
15 Drumsheugh Gardens
Edinburgh EH3 7UG
0131 777 4050 (helpline)

www.inlandrevenue.gov.uk (home pages download leaflets free of charge)

www.inlandrevenue.gov.cto.iht.htm (Inheritance tax)

Law Society of Scotland
26 Drumsheugh Gardens
Edinburgh EH3 7YR
0131 226 7411 (Head Office) 0870 545554
www.lawscot.org.uk

Registers of Scotland
Customer Service Centre
Erskine House
68 Queen Street
Edinburgh EH2 4NF

Or

Registers of Scotland

Customer Service Centre
9 George Square
Glasgow G2 1DY
Tel 0845 6070163
www.ros.gov.uk

Sheriff Clerks Office

Commissary Department
27 Chambers Street
Edinburgh EH1 1LB
0131 225 2525

Appendix 1 Example of Administration Accounts

In the Estate of   Deceased.
Date of death

CAPITAL ACCOUNT

Assets

House Net sales proceeds (value at death £155,000)	£145,000
Less mortgage	£95,000
	£50,000
Stocks and shares (value at death £86500)	£89,000
Life policy	£7500
Skipton BS deposit	£9000
Interest to date of death	£75
National Savings – Premium bonds	£7000
Arrears of pension	£325
Agreed value of house contents	£3800
Car	£5600
Gross estate	£172,300

Less debts and liabilities

Funeral costs	£2000
Gas	£270
Electricity	£25
Administration expenses	£45
Probate fees	£130
Stockbrokers valuation fee	£250
Income tax paid to date of death	£650

Inheritance tax paid on application for probate (N/a) estate less than £316,000

Net Estate carried to distribution account

£168930

For the estate to attract inheritance tax the value would need to be above £316,000. If that is the case, carry on the calculation for inheritance tax by multiplying the residue after £316,000 by 40% which will give you the inheritance tax due.

In the estate of   Deceased

Income account

Dividends received for period from 1st October 2007 to 5th April 2008

Holding	Company	Net dividend
5000 shares	ABC PLC	£1400
4300 shares	Halifax PLC	£560
12000 shares	GKN	£1420
3760 shares	Powergen	£420

Savings accounts final interest   £150

Balance transferred to distribution account

        _____

       £3950

In the estate of   Deceased

Distribution account

Balance transferred from capital account   £168930

Balance transferred from income account   £3950

        _____

        £172880

Less payment of legacies
David Peters   £5000

        _____

Net residuary estate for distribution   £167880
Mr Frederick Dillon
A one half share represented by
  a) House contents   £3800
  b) The balance   £80140
Stella Donaldson
One half share represented by the balance   £83940

Total
£167880

Appendix 2 Sample Last Will and Testament

Sample Last Will and Testament

This is the last Will and Testament

Of   me_____   of

(address)_____

Made this_____ day of_____2009

1. I hereby revoke all former wills and testamentary dispositions heretofore made by me.

2. I appoint (executors and trustees) (hereinafter called "my trustees" which expression where the context admits includes any trustee or trustees hereof for the time being whether original or substituted) to be the executors and trustees thereof and I declare that any of my trustees being a solicitor or other profession shall be entitled to charge accordingly.

3. I appoint_____

4. Of_____
To be the guardian after the death of my wife husband_____ of any of my children who may then be minors.

4. If my wife or husband survives me by thirty days (but not otherwise) I give to him or her absolutely (Subject to payment of debts and other expenses) all my estate both real and personal whatsoever and wheresoever not hereby or by any codicil hereto otherwise specifically disposed of.

5. If my wife or husband as stated in this will is not living at my death the following provisions shall have effect:

I give all my estate both real and personal whatsoever and wheresoever not hereby or any codicil hereto otherwise specifically disposed of unto my trustees UPON TRUST to raise and discharge my debts and funeral and testamentary expenses and all legacies given hereby or by any codicil hereto and any and all taxes payable by reason of my death in respect of property given free of tax and subject thereto UPON TRUST to pay and divide the same equally between my children

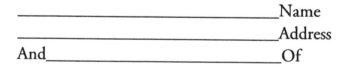

_____Name
_____Address
And_____Of

_____

as shall survive me and attain the age of 18 years provided always that if any child of mine shall die before reaching 18 yrs or marry under that age leaving a child or children such last such last mentioned child or children shall take by substitution and if more than one in equal shares the share of my estate which his or her or their parent would have taken if he or she had survived me.

6. If neither my wife/husband nor children nor any of their issue are living at my death then I give all my estate, both real and personal whatsoever and wheresoever unto my trustees upon trust to raise and discharge thereout my debts and funeral and testamentary expenses and all legacies given hereby or by any codicil hereto and any and all taxes payable by reason of my death in respect of property given free of tax, and subject thereto UPON TRUST to pay and divide the same equally between:

_____Names

of_____ _____Address

7. My Trustees shall have the following powers in addition to their general law powers:
a) to apply for the benefit of any beneficiary as my trustees think fit the whole or any part of the income from that part of my estate to which he is entitled or may in future be entitled.

b) to apply for the benefit of any beneficiary as my trustee thinks fit the whole or any part of the capital to which that beneficiary is entitled.
c) to exercise the power of appropriation conferred by section 41 of The Administration of Estates Act 1925 without obtaining

any of the consents required by that section even though one or more of them may be beneficially interested.

d) to invest trust money and transpose investment with the same full and unrestricted freedom in their choice of investments as if they were an absolute beneficial owner and to apply trust money at any time and from time to time in the purchase with vacant possession or in the improvement of any freehold or leasehold house and to permit the same to be used by any person or person having an interest or prospective interest in my residuary estate upon such terms and conditions from time to time as my trustees in their absolute discretion may think fit.

e) To insure from loss or damage from fire or any other risk any property for the time being comprised in my residuary estate to any amount and even though a person is absolutely entitled to the property and to pay all premiums as due and any insurances out of the income or capital of my residuary estate.

8. I wish my body to be buried_____

In witness to this document I set my hand this _____day of_____2009
Signed by said
witness_____Name
Signature_____

www.straightforwardco.co.uk

All titles, listed below, in the Straightforward Guides Series can be purchased online, using credit card or other forms of payment by going to www.straightfowardco.co.uk A discount of 25% per title is offered with online purchases.

Law
A Straightforward Guide to:
Consumer Rights
Bankruptcy Insolvency and the Law
Employment Law
Private Tenants Rights
Family law
Small Claims in the County Court
Contract law
Intellectual Property and the law
Divorce and the law
Leaseholders Rights
The Process of Conveyancing
Knowing Your Rights and Using the Courts
Producing Your own Will
Housing Rights
The Bailiff the law and You
Probate and The Law
Company law
What to Expect When You Go to Court
Guide to Competition Law
Give me Your Money-Guide to Effective Debt Collection

Caring for a Disabled Child
General titles
Letting Property for Profit
Buying, Selling and Renting property
Buying a Home in England and France
Bookkeeping and Accounts for Small Business
Creative Writing
Freelance Writing
Writing Your own Life Story
Writing performance Poetry
Writing Romantic Fiction
Speech Writing
Teaching Your Child to Read and write
Teaching Your Child to Swim
Raising a Child-The Early Years
Creating a Successful Commercial Website
The Straightforward Business Plan
The Straightforward C.V.
Successful Public Speaking
Handling Bereavement
Play the Game-A Compendium of Rules
Individual and Personal Finance
Understanding Mental Illness
The Two Minute Message
Guide to Self Defence
Buying a Used Car
Tiling for Beginners
Go to: www.straightforwardco.co.uk